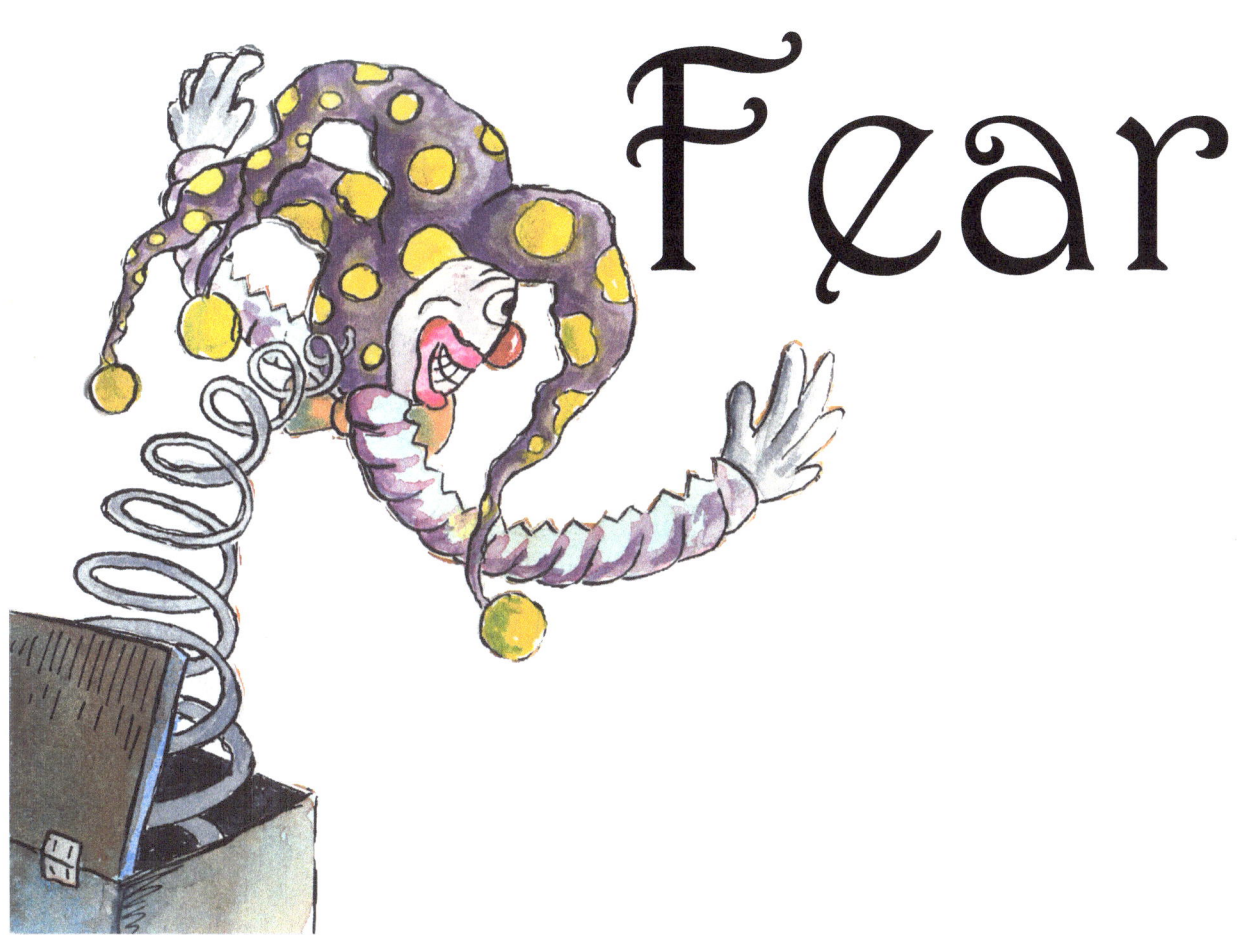

Fear

September 2011

ISBN 978-0-9843838-3-2

Magai New Media, LLC

P.O. Box 740

Rumson, NJ 07760-0740

www.magai.com

Dedicated to Gold Star Mothers.

Thank you for having raised

Heroes with Valor and Honor.

Art / Zack Spakowski

Verse / Bhaskara Rao Achyuthuni

As an infant,
I feared
the absence of my mother

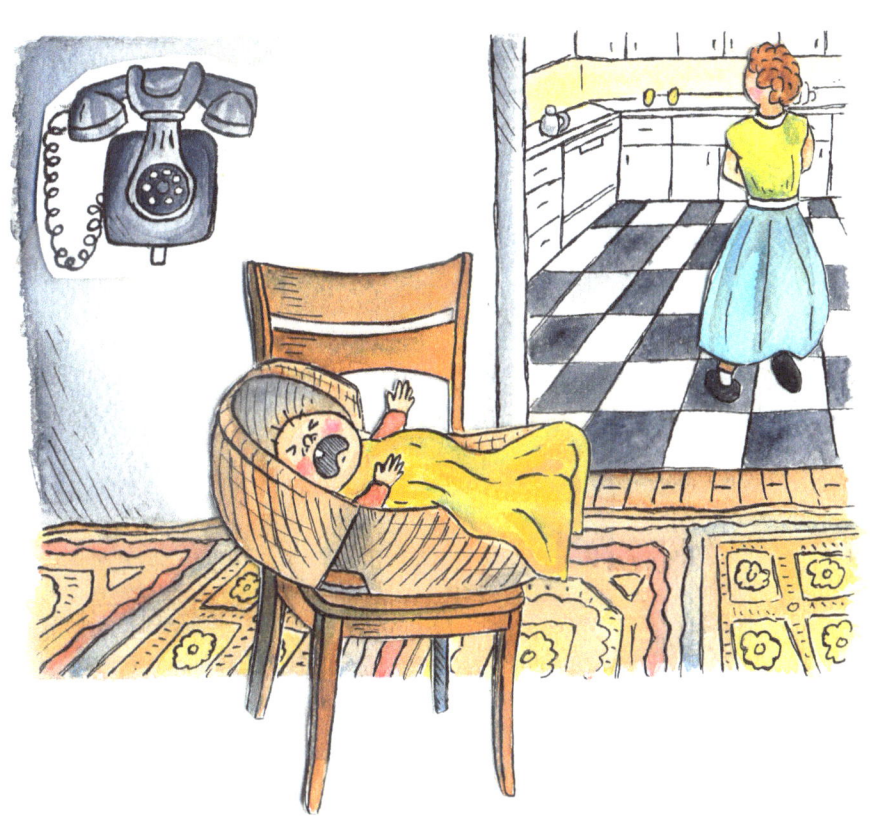

As a toddler,
I feared
the unfamiliar

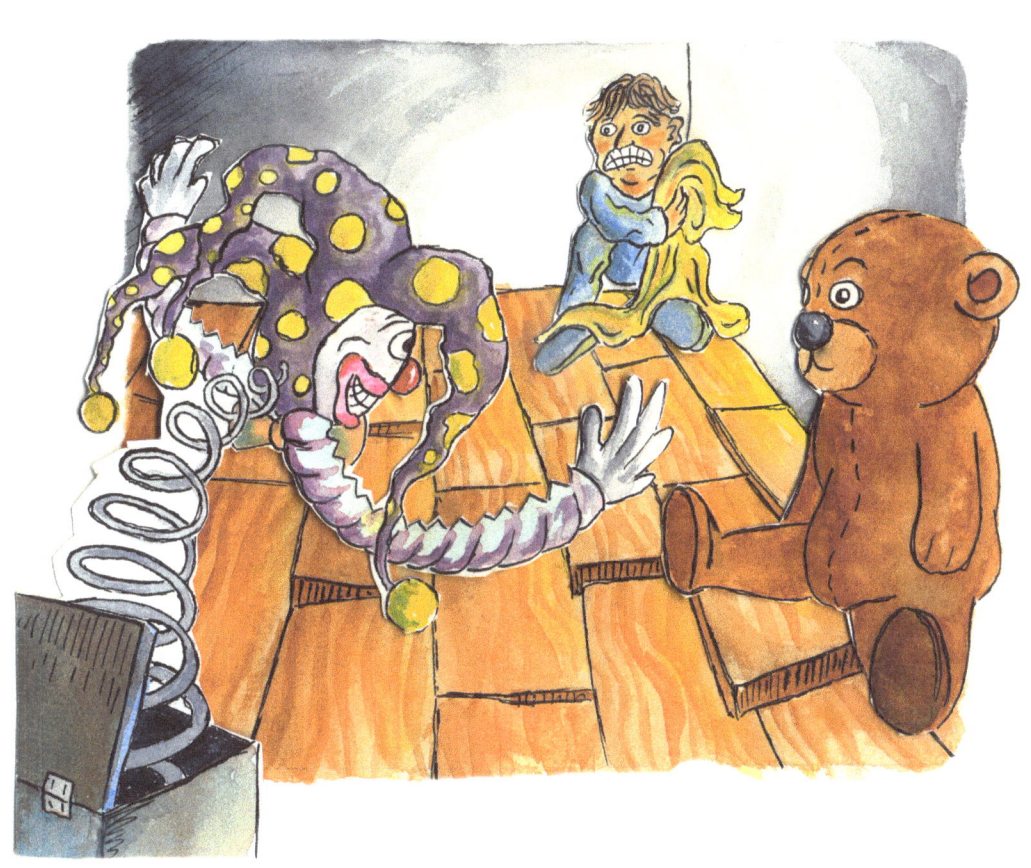

As a child,
I feared
monsters, ghosts
and goblins

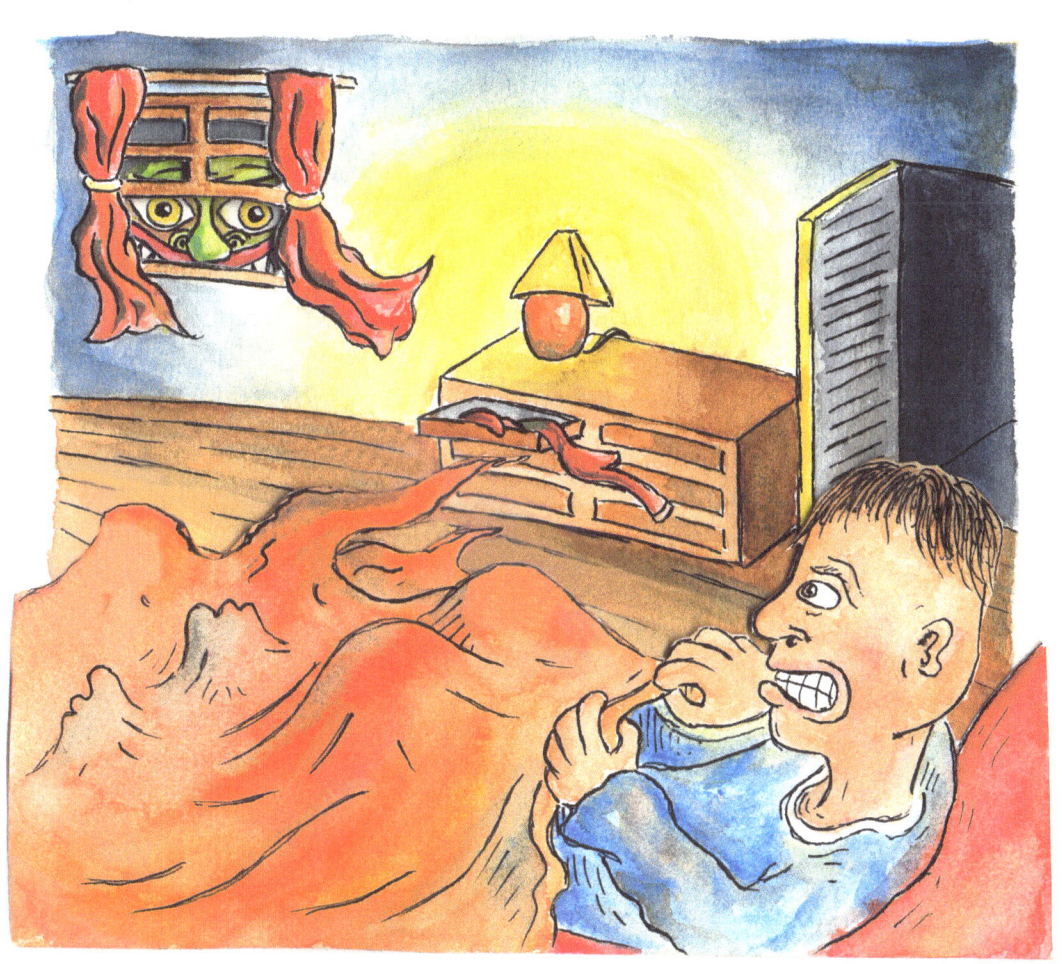

As a student,
I feared
incomprehension

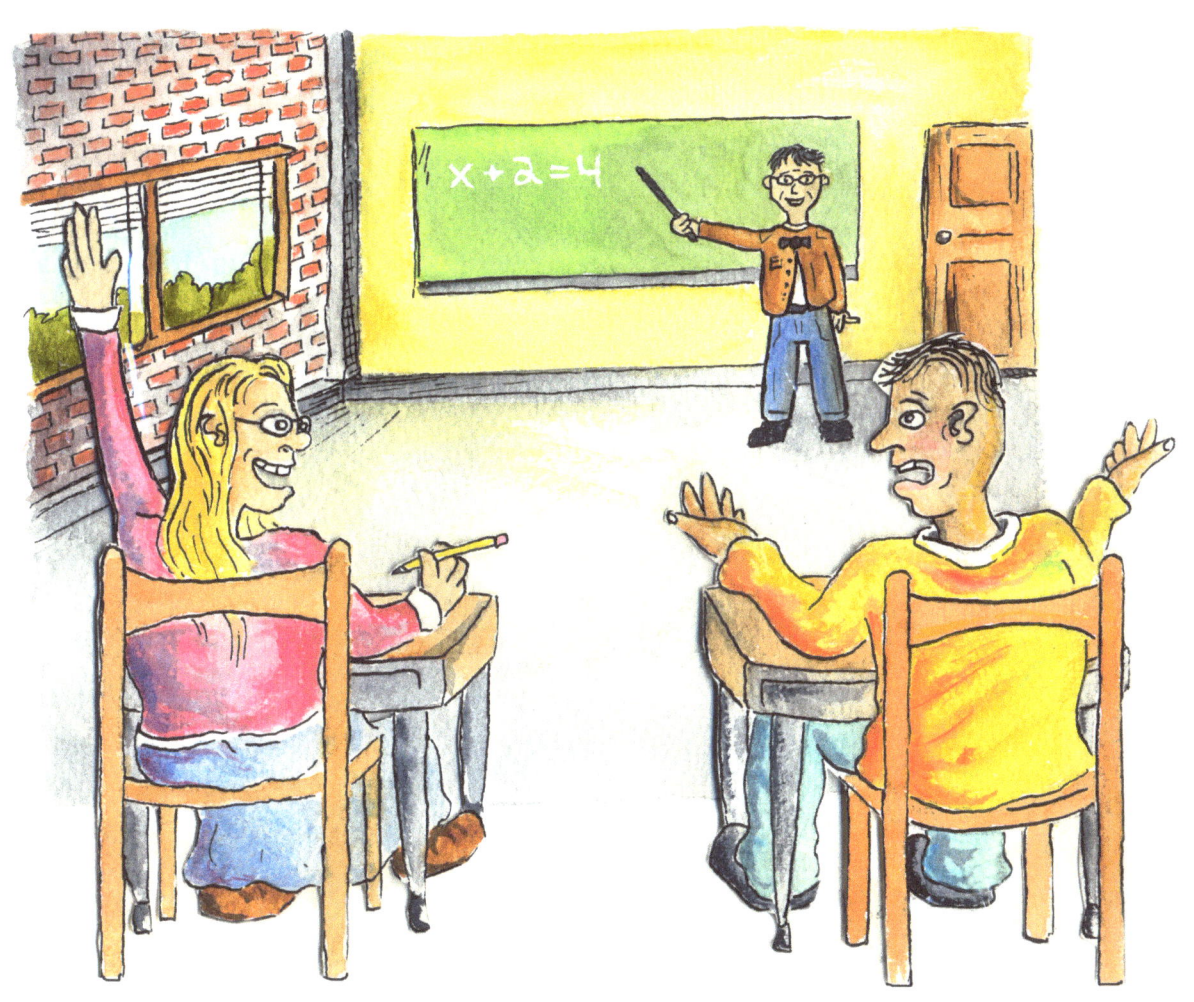

As a friend,
I feared
betrayal

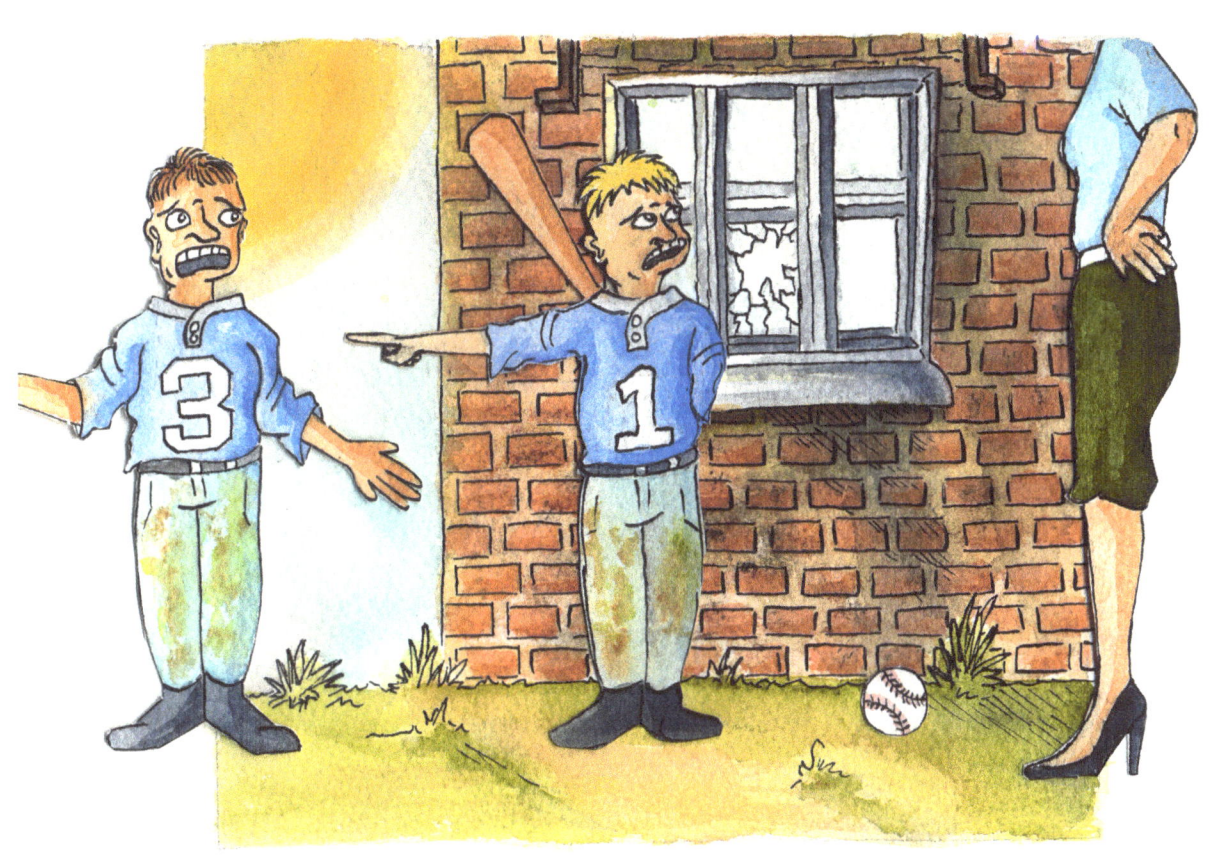

As an adolescent,
I feared
rejection

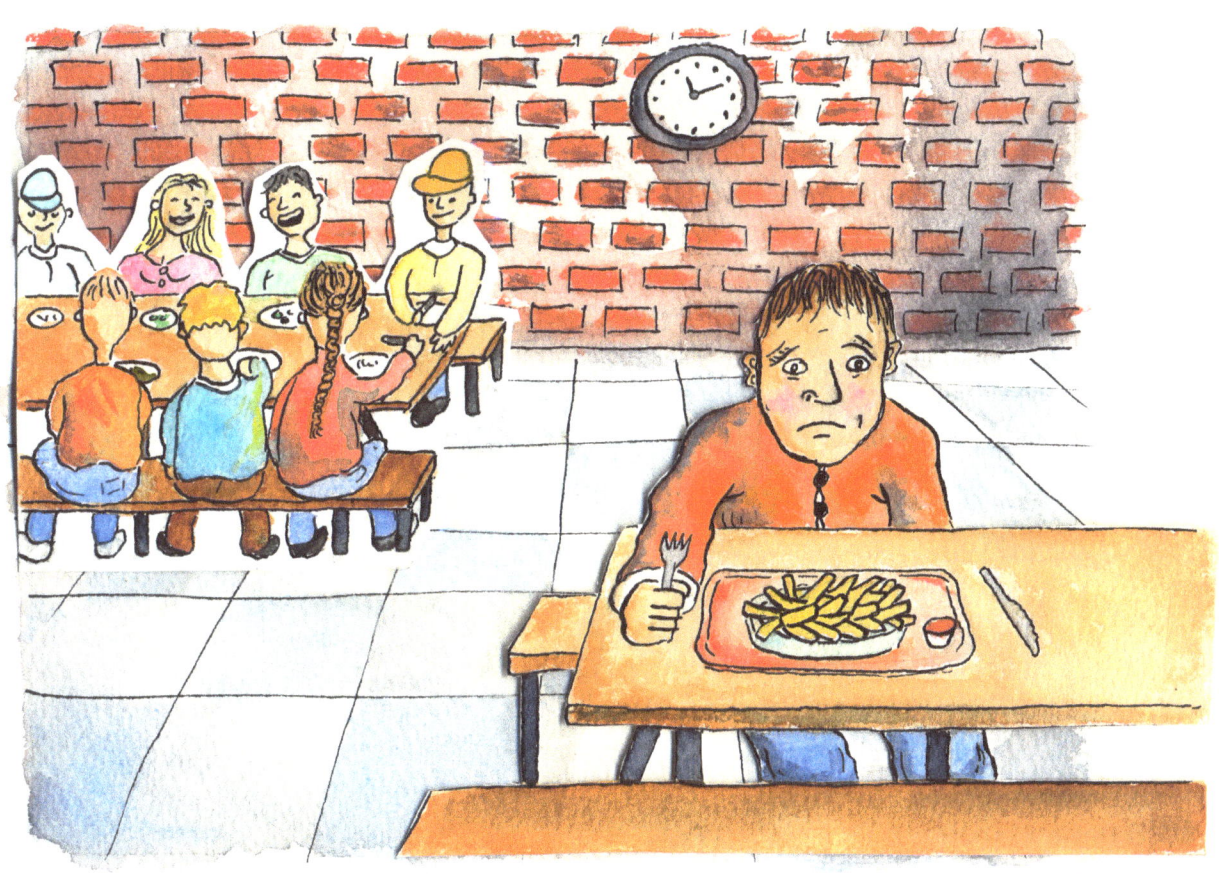

As a worker,
I feared
incompetence

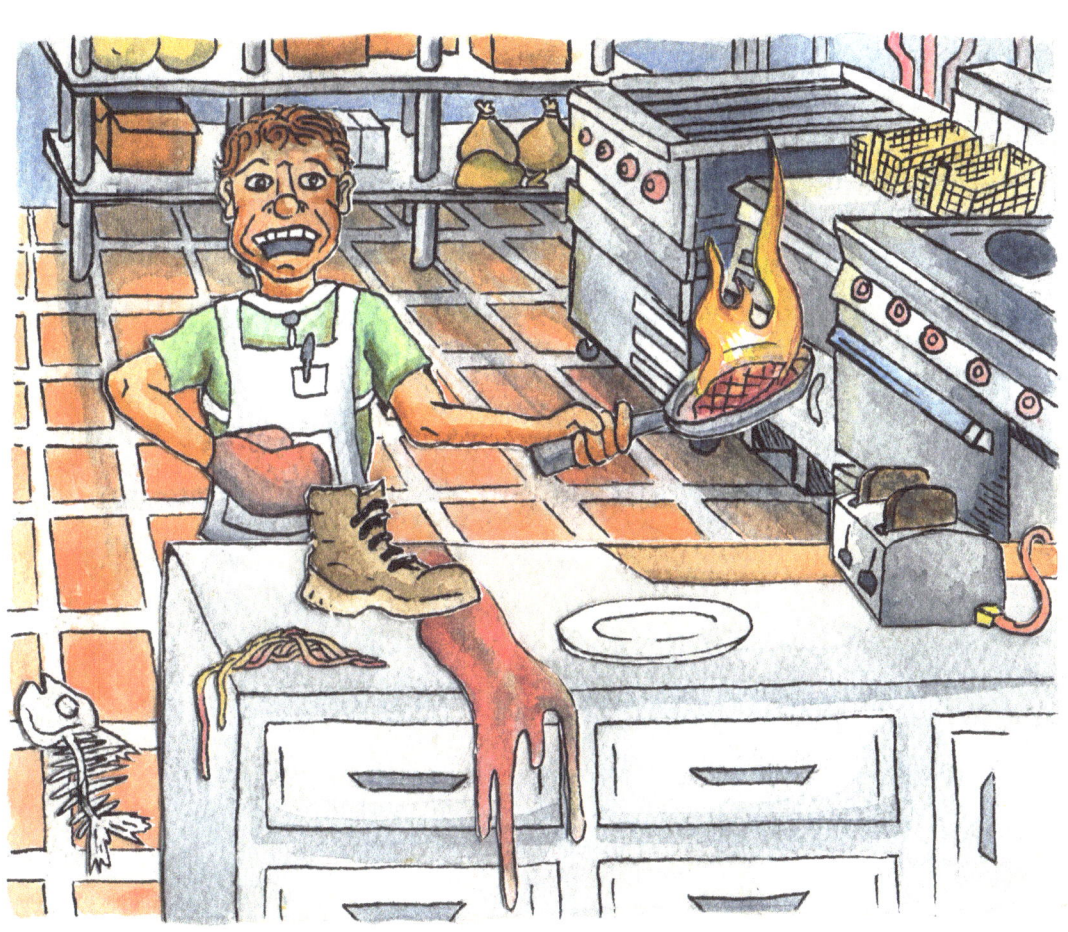

As a soldier,
I feared
cowardice

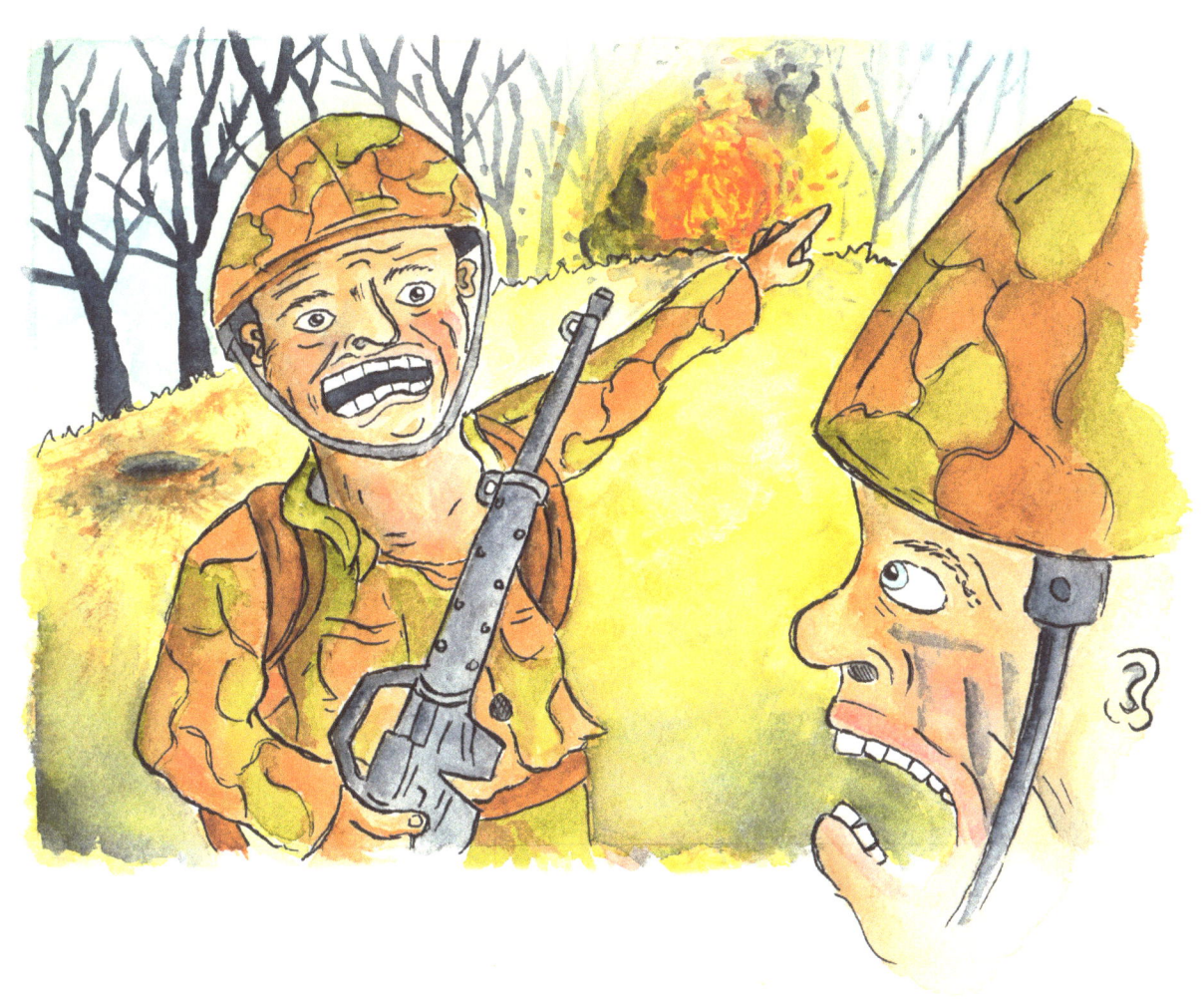

As a lover,
I feared
inadequacy

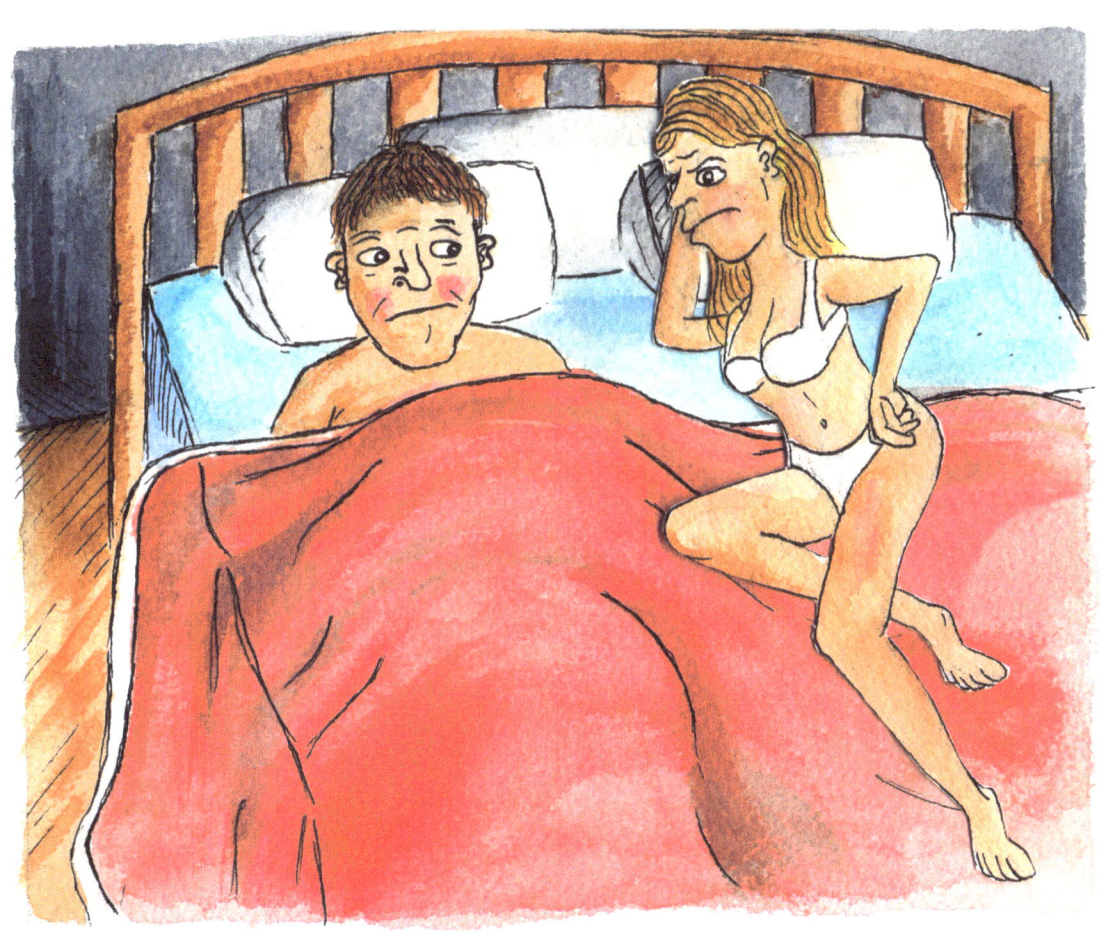

As a parishioner,
I feared
faithlessness

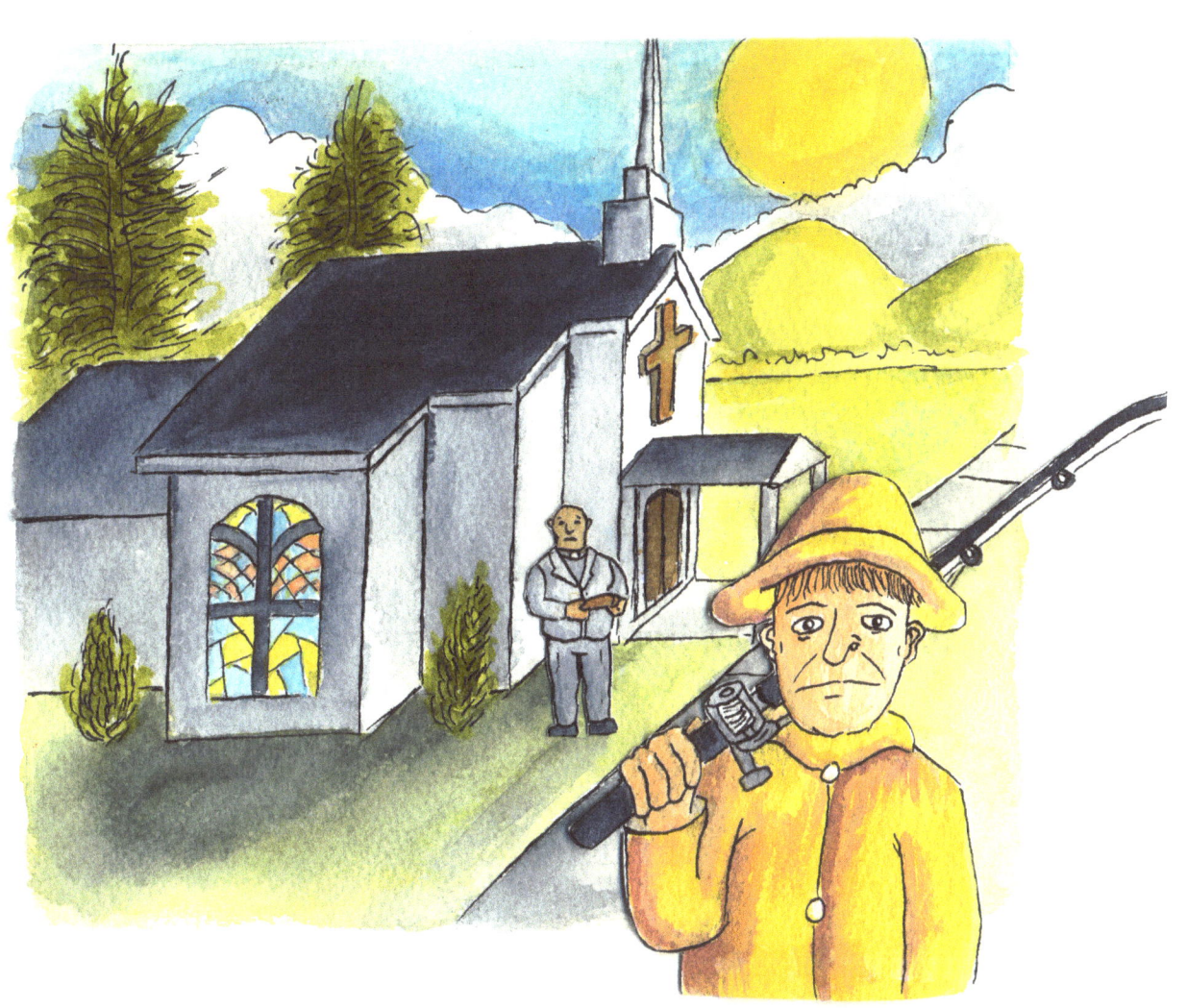

As a spouse,
I feared
infidelity

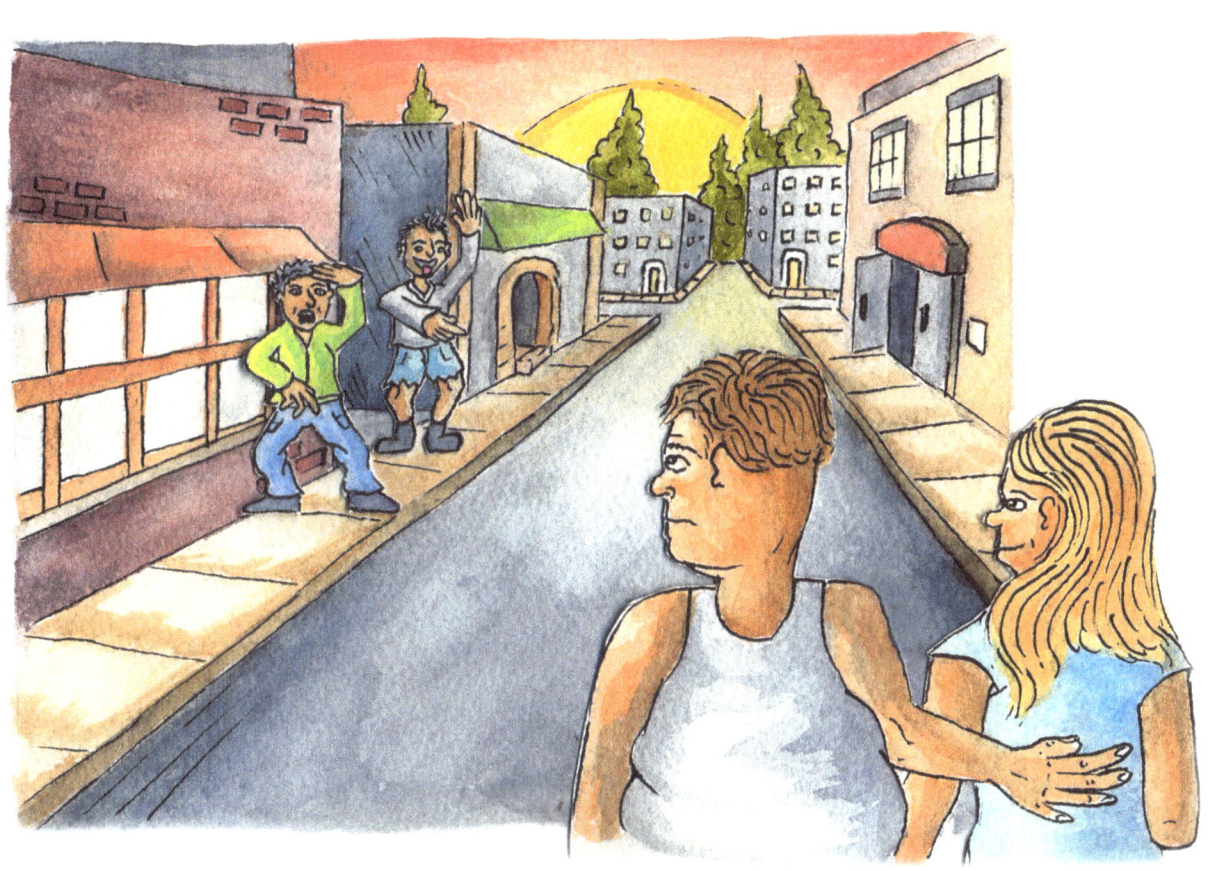

As a neighbor,
I feared
loss of face

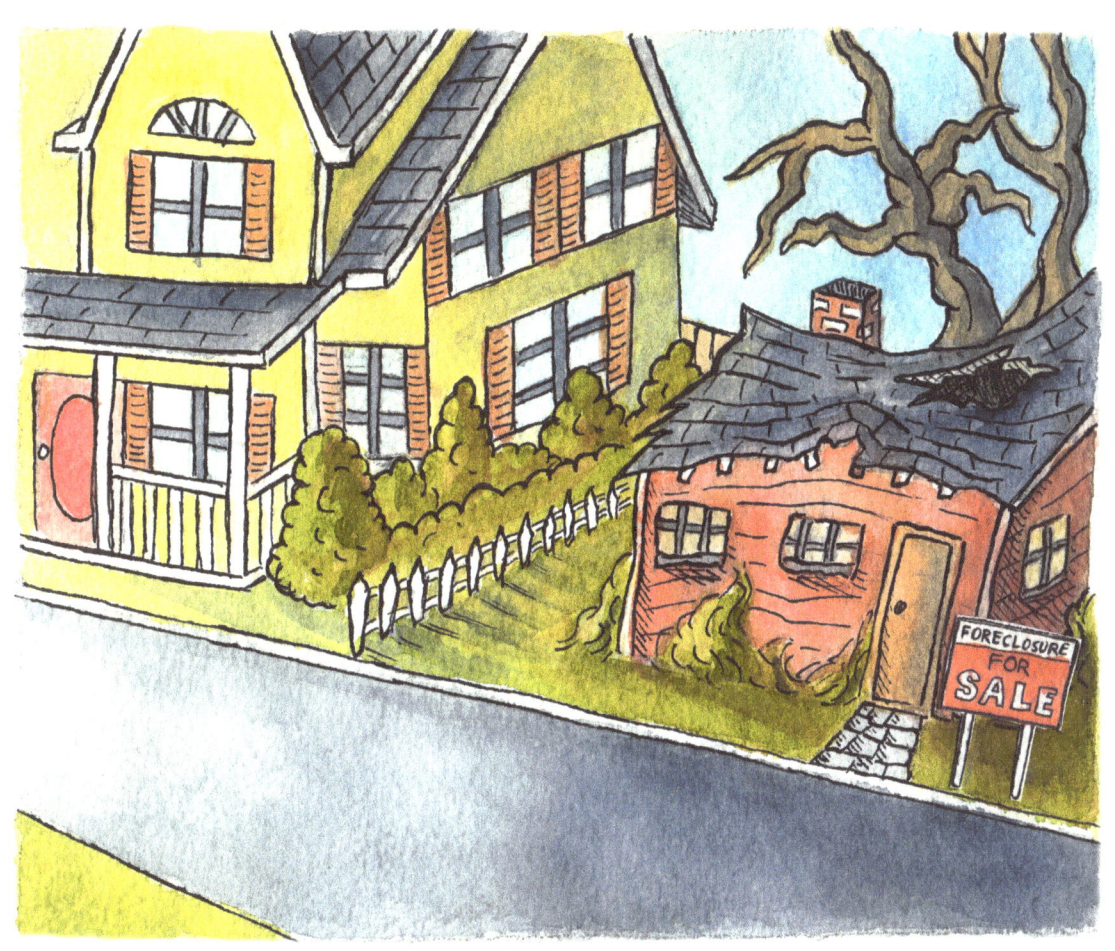

As a parent,
I feared
the loss of a child

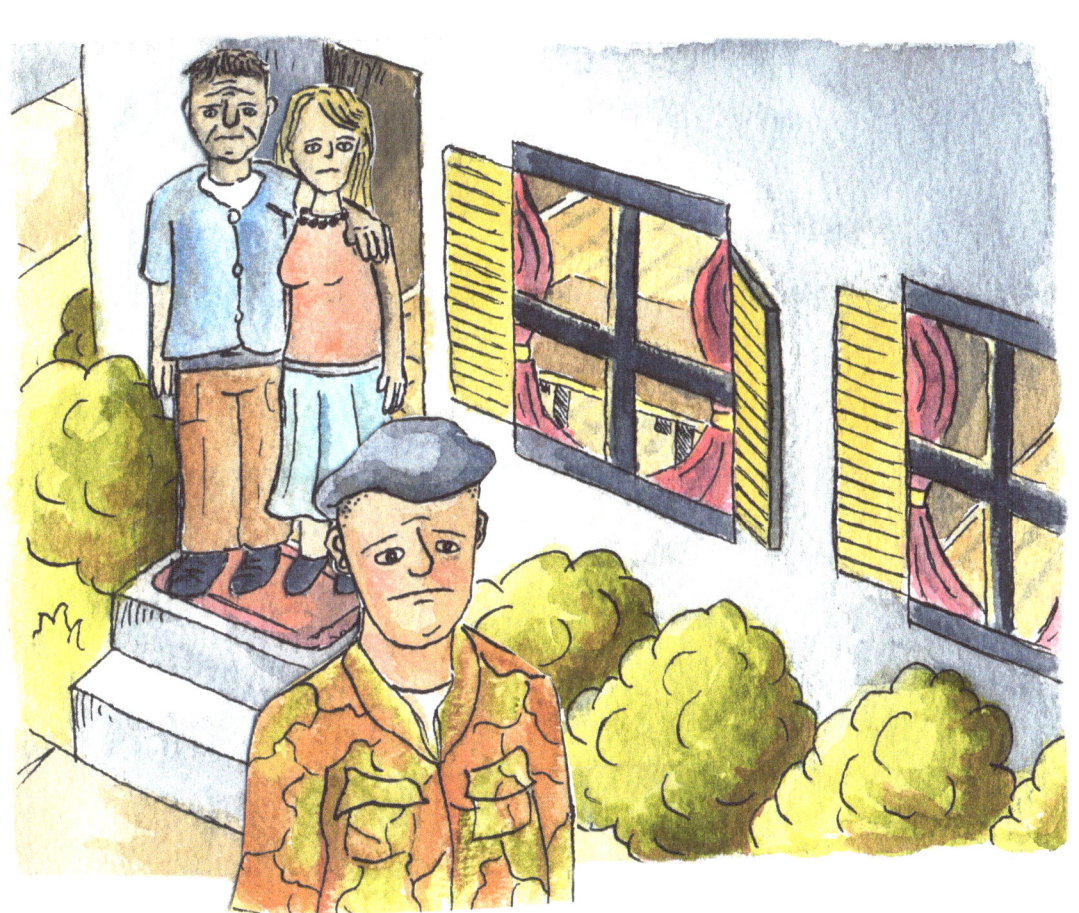

As a retiree,
I feared
uncertainty

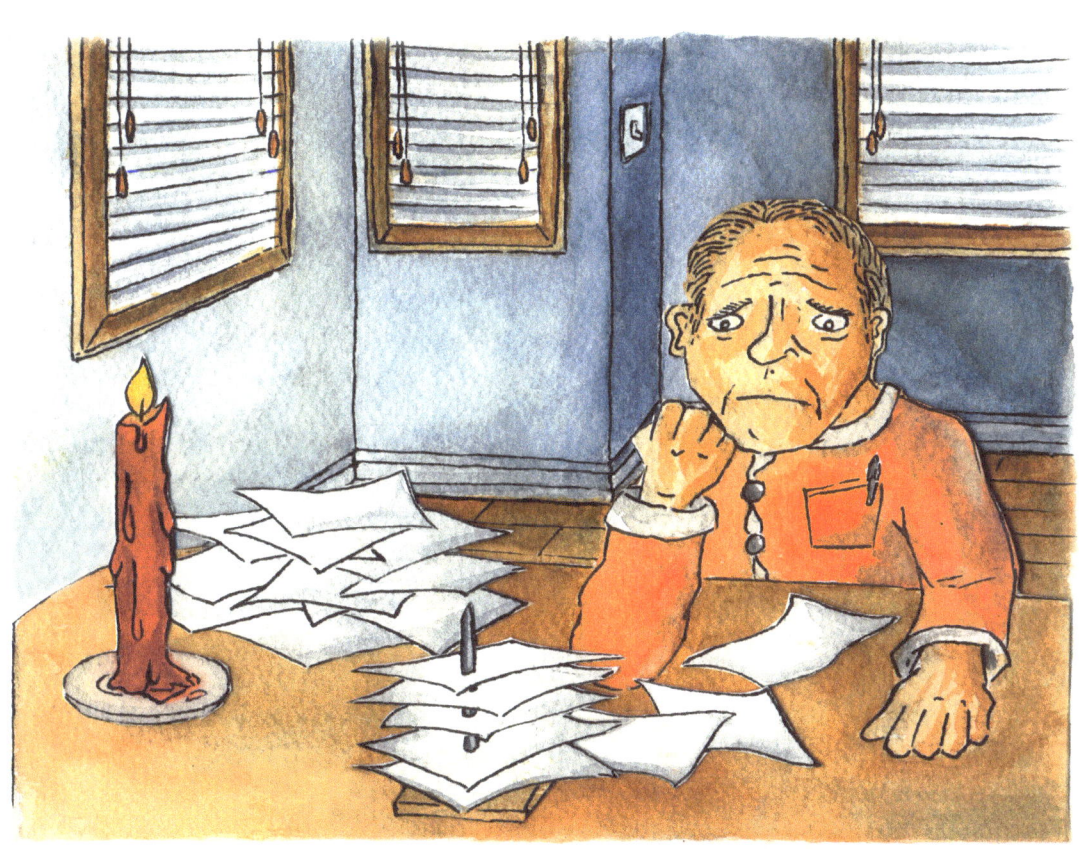

As I prepare
for my final sleep,
I fathom that all my life,
I have feared fear,
and have succumbed
to its tyranny

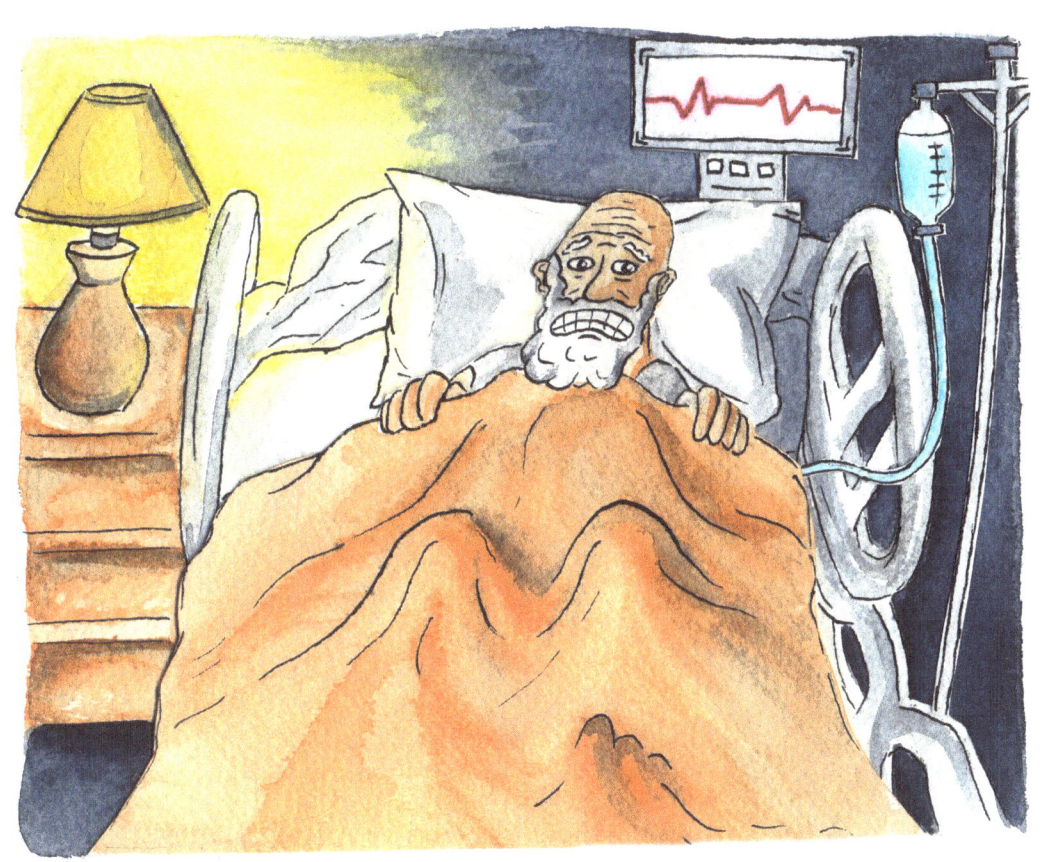

I no longer fear

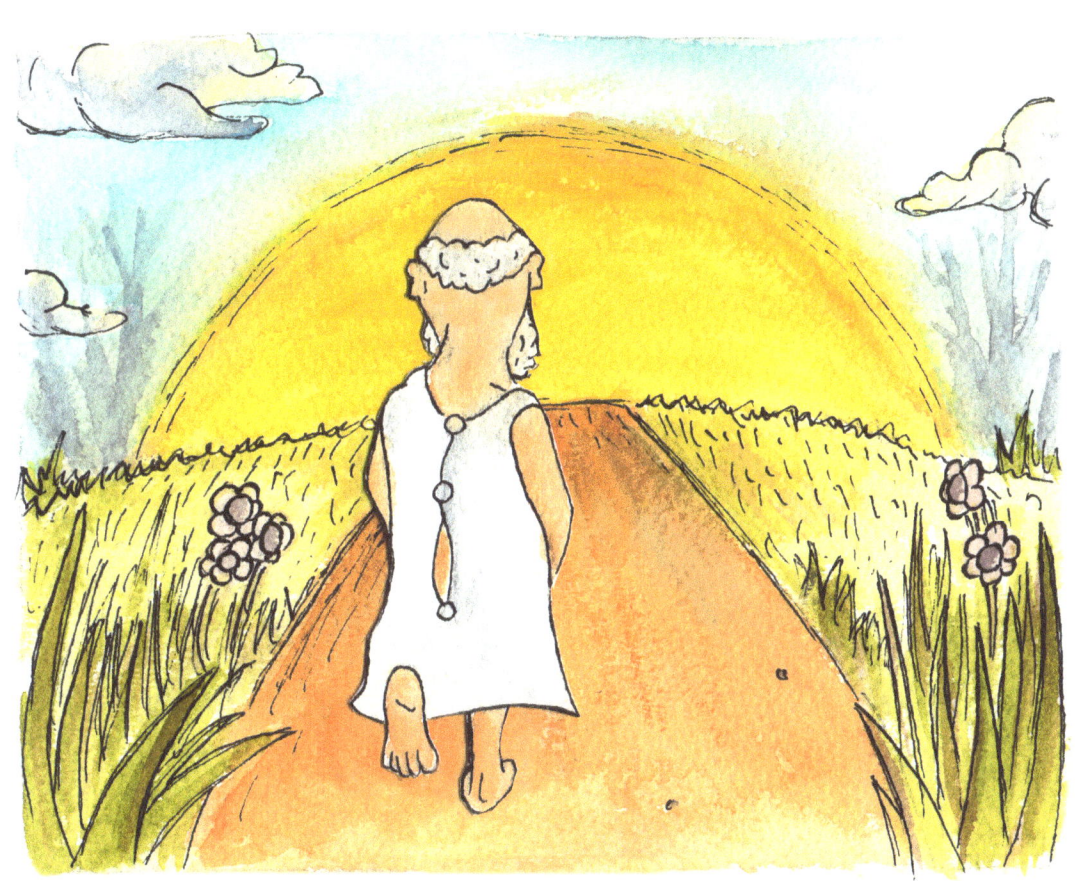

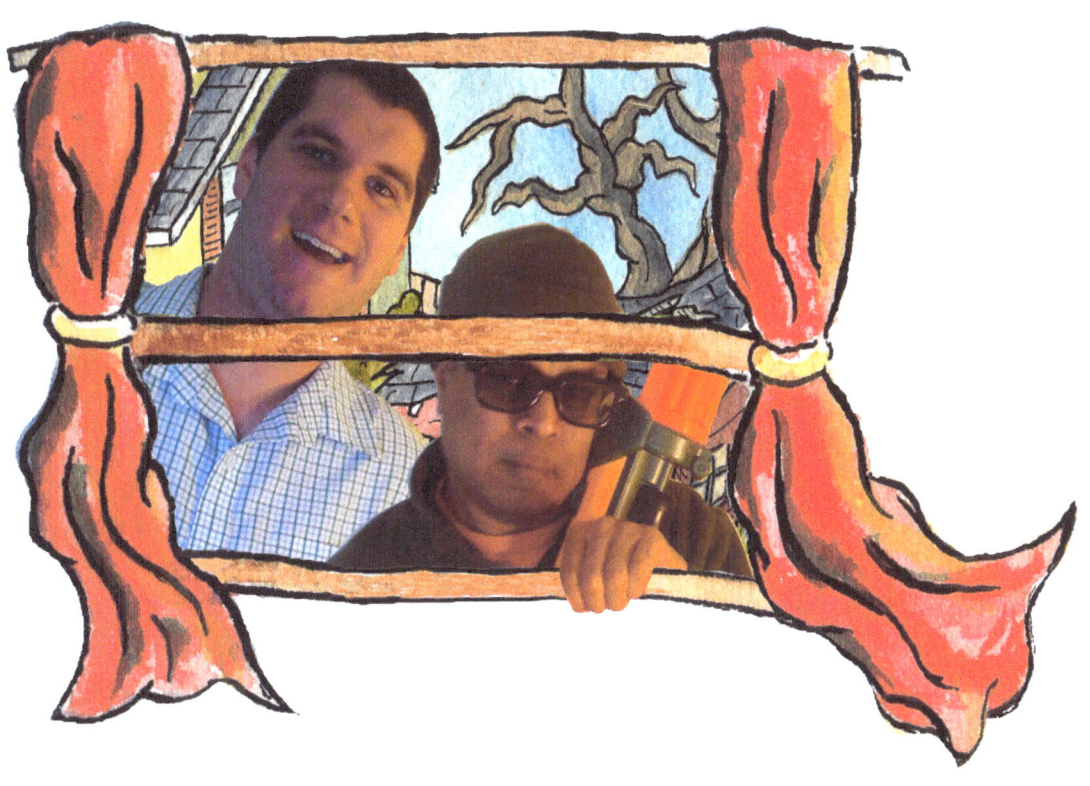

www.ingramcontent.com/pod-product-compliance
Lightning Source LLC
Chambersburg PA
CBHW050357180526
45159CB00005B/2057